Mastering Recursion

Unlocking the Power of Advanced Coding

Table of Contents

1. Introduction 1

2. Unpacking Recursion: An Introduction 2

   2.1. Definition 2

   2.2. Approach 2

   2.3. Essentials of Recursion 3

   2.4. Recursion in Programming Languages 3

   2.5. What's to Come? 4

3. Understanding Base Cases: The Bricks of Recursion 5

   3.1. Understanding the Role of Base Cases 5

   3.2. Constructing the Base Case 5

   3.3. The Importance of a Well-Defined Base Case 6

   3.4. Tweaking Base Cases: Advanced Techniques 7

4. Deep Dive: Recursive Calls and Stack Frames 8

   4.1. Understanding Recursive Calls 8

   4.2. Delving into Stack Frames 9

   4.3. Memory Implications of Stack Frames 11

5. Tracebacks & Debugging Recursive Functions 12

   5.1. Understanding Tracebacks 12

   5.2. Debugging Recursive Functions 13

   5.3. Exceptions and Error Handling with Recursion 14

6. Exploring Tail Recursion and its Optimization 17

   6.1. Understanding Tail Recursion 17

   6.2. From Recursion to Tail Recursion 18

   6.3. Optimization and Tail Call Optimization (TCO) 19

   6.4. Conclusion 20

7. Divide & Conquer: Recursion in Algorithmic Problem Solving . . . 21

   7.1. Unveiling the Strategy of Divide and Conquer 21

   7.2. The Epitome of Divide and Conquer: The Merge Sort

Algorithm 22

7.3. Setting the Stage: Base Cases and Recursive Cases 23

7.4. Recursion and Memory: A Trade-Off to Consider 23

7.5. Unraveling Tail Recursion 24

7.6. Wrapping It Up 24

8. Advanced Recursive Patterns 26

8.1. Understanding the Base Case 26

8.2. Recursive Tree 27

8.3. The Two Forms of Recursion 27

8.4. Multiple Recursive Calls 28

8.5. Space and Time Complexity in Recursive Algorithms 28

8.6. Dynamic Programming and Memoization 29

8.7. Backtracking 29

8.8. Understanding Recursive Paradigms 30

8.9. Exploring Recursive Traversals and Searches 30

9. Real-world Applications of Recursion 31

9.1. Mathematical Problems 31

9.1.1. Factorial 31

9.1.2. Fibonacci Series 32

9.2. Search Algorithms 32

9.2.1. Depth-First Search 32

9.2.2. Binary Search 33

9.3. Fractals 33

9.3.1. Koch Snowflake 33

9.4. Data Structures 34

9.4.1. Binary Trees 34

9.4.2. Linked Lists 34

10. Infinite Recursion: Risks, Issues and Solutions 36

10.1. Understanding Infinite Recursion 36

10.2. The Perils of Infinite Recursion 37

10.3. Spotting Infinite Recursion 37

10.4. Mitigating the Risks 38

11. Looking Ahead: Recursion in Contemporary Programming Languages 40

11.1. Java and Recursion 40

11.2. C++ and Recursion 41

11.3. JavaScript and Recursion 41

11.4. Python and Recursion 42

11.5. Haskell and Recursion 43

Chapter 1. Introduction

In this Special Report titled "Mastering Recursion: Unlocking the Power of Advanced Coding", we delve deep into the labyrinthine yet fascinating world of recursive programming. This is not your typical light reading, but a carefully designed guide crafted to untangle the complexities of recursion—an advanced coding concept that is, often, undeniably intimidating. Fear not, for we gently guide you on your journey, breaking down the intricate concepts into palatable nuggets, expelling any apprehension you may harbor. Whether you're a seasoned programmer seeking to refine your skills or a curious beginner venturing into the wilderness of code, this report is your indispensable companion. We make sure that by the end of it, you won't just understand recursion—you will have mastered it! Herein lay the keys to uncap powerful computation possibilities, driven by the magic of recursion. The world of advanced coding awaits. Buckle in, step up, and let curiosity lead the way!

Chapter 2. Unpacking Recursion: An Introduction

There's a popular joke among computer science enthusiasts that reads, "In order to understand recursion, one must first understand recursion." Sardonic as it may be, this quip captures the essence of recursion, a mesmerizing concept in the world of programming.

Before plunging headfirst into the real crux of recursion, it's imperative to frame an ideal setting by duly acknowledging the terms involved.

2.1. Definition

Recursion, defined in the simplest terms, is a process in which a function calls itself as a subroutine. It's a concept that inherently applies to both computer science and mathematics where it's used to solve problems or define functions in a self-referential manner. Another comparable example could be nested Matryoshka dolls, where each doll is a smaller version of the previous one; the entire structure is a doll, and yet each single piece is also a doll.

2.2. Approach

In principle, recursion is a method of solving complicated problems by breaking them down into more manageable sub-problems of the same type. It's the computer science equivalent of the adage "divide and conquer." By continually whittling our problem down to a more digestible size, we can solve even the most complex of issues. The pivotal aspect however, is having the base case—an elementary instance of the problem that can be solved directly. Recursive algorithms converge towards these base cases.

Now, with a broad understanding of what recursion embodies, we can journey deeper, systematically untangling the intricate web of recursion.

2.3. Essentials of Recursion

Embracing recursion involves comprehending its two cardinal rules - the base condition and the recursive step, often depicted as the 'termination scenario' and the 'redux process', respectively.

Every recursive function must have a condition to stop calling itself. Failure to define this condition results in an infinite loop, making the program crash eventually due to a stack overflow.

Once a base case is defined, you could then go on to calling the function recursively to perform the necessary computation, until the base condition holds true, after which the function stops calling itself and begins returning the values up the call stack.

To highlight these concepts, consider the calculation of a factorial. For instance, the factorial of a non-negative integer number 'n' is the product of all positive integers less than or equal to 'n'. You can call the factorials as n! where 'n' is a non-negative integer and is calculated as n * (n-1) * (n-2)...*3 * 2 * 1. The factorial of 0 and 1 is 1.

Given this, a factorial can be defined recursively because the factorial of 'n' can be calculated as the product of 'n' multiplied by the factorial of (n-1) until we reach the base case with n being 0 or 1.

2.4. Recursion in Programming Languages

Recursion can be implemented in many programming languages like Python, C++, Java, JavaScript, and C#. Let's examine some specifics on how recursion is dealt within programming languages.

1. Parameters and Returns: It's not the function itself that is recursive; rather it's the method inside that carries it out. The return statement defines the recursive call and includes the problem that's shrunken with each recursion.

2. Function Stack: The function stack forms the crucial backbone. Every time a recursive call is made, its intermediate workings are saved into a stack, a data structure that works on the principle of LIFO (Last In First Out). When the algorithm eventually hits the base case, it helps construct the answer by using values on top of the stack.

3. Memory Management: Recursion does require effective management of memory resources. We must take heed of the space complexity and the potential for a stack overflow. Keeping track of a large number of recursive calls could halt your system, hence it is important to design the recursions effectively.

A detailed analysis of these factors would be discussed as we delve further into the applications of recursion, its advantages and the potential pitfalls.

2.5. What's to Come?

Though the world of recursion may at first come across like a maze, once you accustom yourself to its transformative power, you'll find a wealth of possibilities at your fingertips. As the exploration of recursion continues, we will start fleshing it out with meaningful examples, illustrations and more intricate concepts.

Remember, the key to mastering recursion is practice and patient understanding. Keep a steady pace, take calculated steps, and open your mind to the fascinating, mind-bending wonders of recursion in coding.

Chapter 3. Understanding Base Cases: The Bricks of Recursion

One of the main hallmarks of recursion is the concept of base cases. Beyond the realm of superficial definitions, let's dive in to comprehend the depths of the base cases.

3.1. Understanding the Role of Base Cases

Base cases play an unmistakable role as the cornerstone of recursion, akin to the foundation in building architecture. A recursive function, without a base case, ventures into an infinite chain of function calls, leading to an inevitable program crash due to a stack overflow error.

Imagine yourself in a seemingly endless maze. To escape this convoluted construct, you decide to follow an algorithm: at every junction, you take the path to the right. If you encounter a dead end or a place you've already been to, you backtrack. This strategy, at its core, is recursive, as the same approach is applied at each step.

However, suppose the maze lacks exit points or dead ends - base cases in our analogy. The algorithm would trap you in an infinite loop, forever wandering in the twisted labyrinth, akin to a recursive function that keeps calling itself, leading to a stack overflow.

3.2. Constructing the Base Case

A base case is essentially a set of condition(s), which when satisfied, terminates the recursion. To construct the base case, identify the simplest instance of the problem, a scenario so basic that the answer is known without any additional computations or function calls.

Consider the classical example of calculating factorial using recursion. The factorial of a number n (denoted by n!) is the product of all positive integers less than or equal to n. However, when n equals 0 or 1, we instantly know that the factorial is 1. This serves as our base case.

The recursive function for factorial, considering the base case, would look something like this in Python:

```python
def factorial(n):
    if n == 0 or n == 1:      # Base case
        return 1
    else:
        return n * factorial(n-1)     # Recursive call
```

In the first two lines, we define the base case. If n is 0 or 1, the function instantly returns 1.

3.3. The Importance of a Well-Defined Base Case

As we progress deeper into the world of recursion, the relevance of a well-defined base case becomes increasingly evident. A poorly defined base case might not halt the recursion when it should, leading to unnecessary function calls, or it might stop the recursion prematurely, giving incorrect results.

Let's illustrate this with an example. Suppose we're tasked with finding the sum of all positive integers up to n. Defining the sum of numbers up to 0 as the base case (since it's the simplest instance) and stating its value as 0 seems intuitive.

A poorly defined base case for this problem might be to consider 1 as the base case and return 1. In such a scenario, if the function is called with 0 as an argument, it would keep calling itself with -1, -2, -3, and so on, leading to a stack overflow.

The importance of a base case also stems from the fact that it plays a key role in determining the time complexity of a recursive function. Unnecessary recursion levels can turn an efficient solution into a highly inefficient one.

3.4. Tweaking Base Cases: Advanced Techniques

As one gains proficiency in recursive programming, there might arise scenarios where tweaking the base case or having multiple base cases might lead to better performance or a more elegant solution.

For instance, in the problem of calculating the nth Fibonacci number, having two base cases (n=0 return 0 and n=1 return 1), not only makes for a simpler solution but also avoids incorrect results (since the first two Fibonacci numbers are defined as 0 and 1 respectively).

Conclusively, understanding, constructing, and tweaking base cases are fundamental skills in mastering recursion. Armed with appropriately defined base cases, your recursive functions will hold their ground and run efficiently against the problems you set out to solve.

In the subsequent chapters, we will build upon these foundational concepts and introduce some more intricate aspects of recursion. You are now a step closer to mastering the fascinating realm of recursion, so stay tuned for the exciting journey ahead!

Chapter 4. Deep Dive: Recursive Calls and Stack Frames

Recursion in programming is an effulgent methodology where a function calls itself within its body, akin to Russian dolls where each doll is encapsulated progressively within its larger replica. The concept might appear muddled initially, but as we dip our toes into the sea of recursive calls and stack frames, the enigma starts to unfurl, revealing a revelation of computational potency. This intricate dance between recursive calls and stack frames forms the backbone of recursion, a concept that is both exhilarating and groundbreaking when understood entirely.

4.1. Understanding Recursive Calls

To assess the concept of recursive calls, we need to firstly direct our attention towards the humble function. Functions are the building blocks of code—they receive input, process it, and return an output. A recursive call occurs when this function, during the act of processing, invokes itself. This might appear nonsensical at first; after all, how could a function possibly embark on a task only to ask itself to complete the same task again?

Imagine a function responsible for computing the factorial of a number, a popular example often used to elucidate the concept of recursion. The factorial of a number is simply the product of all positive integers less than or equal to the number. For instance, the factorial of 5 or, mathematically written as 5!, is 5 x 4 x 3 x 2 x 1 = 120.

Sure, a factorial could be found using a simple iterative loop, but watch as this process unfolds so elegantly when recursion is used:

```
function factorial(n) {
    if (n === 0) return 1;
    else return n * factorial(n - 1);
}
```

Herein lies the beauty of a recursive call. Our humble factorial function does indeed start by computing the factorial of the number n, yet during this process, it calls itself—this time to compute the factorial of n - 1. This process repeats, tumbling down the hierarchy until n reaches 0 — our base case.

At this point, the function ceases to call itself further and begins to return the outputs back up the calling stack.

Notably, this journey of descending down and climbing back up the ladder of call stack is paramount to recursion.

4.2. Delving into Stack Frames

Every time a function calls itself, it creates what we refer to in computer science as a 'stack frame' or 'activation record'. This stack frame is a treasure trove of information, storing the function's variables, parameters, and return addresses. A unique stack frame is minted with every function call, resulting in a stack of these frames, the control of which is maintained by the call stack.

Detailed understanding of stack frames is crucial to both optimizing recursion and debugging recursive functions. Let's walk you through the working of stack frames with our factorial function example.

When the factorial function receives the input 5, it first checks the condition n === 0. Since 5 is not 0, the function results in the recursive call 5 * factorial(4). At this point, a stack frame is created containing the variables, parameters, and return address of this function call.

The workings of the stack frame look something like this:

```
Stack frame for factorial(5)
---
* Parent address: (address of the previous function or
caller)
* Parameters: n = 5
* Variables: none
* Return address: line 3, after the multiplication
```

The newly created stack frame for factorial(5) is added on top of the call stack. The function then moves onto factorial(4), creating another stack frame:

```
Stack frame for factorial(4)
---
* Parent address: (address of factorial(5))
* Parameters: n = 4
* Variables: none
* Return address: line 3, after the multiplication
```

This process continues, adding stack frames for factorial(3), factorial(2), factorial(1), and finally factorial(0). Once n equals 0, the base case is triggered, marking a turning point in our recursive journey. The function starts returning the results, beginning with factorial(0) returning 1.

By returning the results, the function call completes, and the corresponding stack frame is popped off the call stack. The return addresses stored in the stack frames guide the function back through the chain of calls, multiplying the results as it goes. This unfurling process up the call stack continues until we reach our first call, factorial(5). The result of this recursive adventure, 120, emerges from a chrysalis of recursive calls and stack frames.

4.3. Memory Implications of Stack Frames

Stack frames, while essential for recursion, do consume memory. Every new function call and its corresponding stack frame inevitably takes up space in the memory. When a function goes too deep into recursion, creating numerous stack frames, it could exhaust the stack space. This scenario results in a StackOverflow error, a programmer's nightmare not to be confused with the popular Q&A platform for coders.

Optimizing recursive calls and understanding tail recursion could be the answer to preventing this memory overload. Hence, becoming proficient with recursion necessitates a clear comprehension of the mesmerizing dance between recursive calls and stack frames.

Understanding recursion, like wandering through an Escher painting, leads us back to where we began, but richer in knowledge and perspective. The journey through recursive calls and stack frames might've been complex, but we hope you now find yourself more confident, intrigued, and excited to apply recursion in your coding endeavors. However, this is just the beginning—let's further unravel this potency as we proceed towards mastery!

Chapter 5. Tracebacks & Debugging Recursive Functions

Understanding the inner workings of a recursive function is critical for effective debugging. Once we grasp how these functions behave and move, we can visualize the call stack during each execution.

"How does one go about doing so?" you may wonder. Well, here we get into the domain of tracebacks. In this section, we address the ubiquitous obstacles programmers face while dealing with recursive functions: tracebacks, and subsequent debugging.

5.1. Understanding Tracebacks

Tracebacks are the reports that provide valuable insights into what occurs when a Python error is thrown. They trace back the execution steps revealed by function calls that led right up to the error. Note, these tracebacks are printed out in reverse order, effectively giving you a bottom-up view of your function stack.

An example of a common traceback you might face when working with recursion is the "RecursionError: maximum recursion depth exceeded." Python limits the depth of recursion to help avoid infinite recursion or exceeding your system's stack limit.

```python
def recursive_function():
    recursive_function()

recursive_function()
```

The preceding infinite recursion will result in a "RecursionError" as your function will call itself indefinitely, exceeding Python's maximum recursion depth. The traceback would look something like this:

```
RecursionError: maximum recursion depth exceeded
```

This traceback reveals that we've ventured too deep into recursion. Python is usually set up with a recursion limit of about 1000, though this can vary between systems and configurations.

5.2. Debugging Recursive Functions

Understanding a traceback is only one part of the equation when it comes to mastering recursion. As you navigate your way, you'll need to debug your functions. Debugging is the process of identifying and fixing issues in your code. There are several techniques and tools you can use to make debugging easier:

1. Print Statements: Print statements can be useful in tracing how your function behaves at each step of execution. You can print out the values of arguments at each recursive call and the return values at each step.

2. Debuggers: Python comes with a built-in debugger, pdb. It's a little more advanced tool than print statements, enabling you to pause your program, inspect the values of variables, and step through your program line by line.

Let's look at an example using pdb:

```python
import pdb

def factorial(n):
    pdb.set_trace()
    if n == 1:
```

```python
        return 1
    else:
        return n * factorial(n - 1)


print(factorial(5))
```

When you run this script, you will see the pdb prompt showing the current execution line. You can use the command `args` to see the current variable values, `step` to step into the next function call, or `next` to go to the next line in the current function.

Using pdb, or any debugger for that matter, will significantly improve your understanding of the intricate flow of recursive functions.

1. Visualization Tools: Lastly, there are online tools, like Python Tutor, that can run your code and visually represent the function calls and variables. These can be incredibly helpful for getting an intuitive grasp of recursion.

5.3. Exceptions and Error Handling with Recursion

Apart from debugging, a key part of mastering recursion is handling exceptions correctly. Error handling helps ensure your program behaves predictably and provides informative error messages when things go wrong.

Python uses a model of exceptions for error handling. When a function encounters an error, it can raise an exception. A higher-level function can either handle this exception (with try-except) or allow it to propagate upwards.

Consider a recursive function without proper error handling:

```python
def countdown(n):
    if n <= 0:
        raise Exception("Number should be positive")
    elif n == 1:
        print(n)
    else:
        print(n)
        countdown(n - 1)
```

In this example, a negative number will cause the function to raise
an unhandled exception. To make our function more robust, we can
add exception handling:

```python
def countdown(n):
    try:
        if n <= 0:
            raise Exception("Number should be positive")
        elif n == 1:
            print(n)
        else:
            print(n)
            countdown(n - 1)
    except Exception as e:
        print(f"Error: {e}")
```

Just like ensuring your recursive function's base case is reachable,
you need to make sure your errors are appropriate and handled
correctly.

The nuances of tracebacks, debugging, and error handling with
recursion open the door to fully understanding and employing
recursion to solve complex problems. These form the foundations to
navigating the labyrinth of recursion. Further on, we will delve
deeper into recursion's uses and limitations, tuning your abilities all

the way from understanding recursion to mastering it.

Navigating the labyrinth of recursion may seem daunting at first, but with perseverance, practice, and with your mind armed with tracebacks and debugging, you will, inevitably, conquer the subtleties of recursion. To master the world of advanced coding is no small feat, but fear not, for you have started on the path. So, strap on your seatbelt, embrace the complexities, and prepare to dive deeper into recursion!

Chapter 6. Exploring Tail Recursion and its Optimization

Tail recursion is a powerful programming concept wrapped in a seemingly innocuous cloak. At a glance, tail recursion could be mistaken for just another form of regular recursion. However, once you understand its essence, you'll appreciate the unique difference it offers in optimizing recursive function operations.

Let's start with a clear-cut definition—tail recursion occurs when a recursive function's last action is a call to itself, meaning the function delegates all its tasks to this last recursive call.

6.1. Understanding Tail Recursion

To illustrate, consider a function in pseudocode:

```
FUNCTION findFactorial(n, factorial=1):
    IF n == 1:
        RETURN factorial
    ELSE:
        RETURN findFactorial(n-1, n*factorial)
```

In the `findFactorial` function provided, the last action is a recursive call to the function itself. Hence, the execution of `findFactorial` is a tail-recursive process.

Tail recursion can dramatically optimize recursive functionality because it removes the need to keep track of previous function calls. How does it do that? Remember that with standard recursion, every recursive call must complete before the next recursive operation can take place. This necessitates extra computational power for maintaining stack frames—a costly affair indeed.

In contrast, tail recursive functions obviate this need. The recursive call is the last operation, implying that the system needn't remember previous states. It simply recalculates all necessary elements within the recursive call and moves on to the next, making it possible to reuse the same stack frame for each recursive call, saving time and space.

6.2. From Recursion to Tail Recursion

You might be wondering: can standard recursive functions convert into tail recursive functions? The answer is yes, within reason. In fact, understanding how to do it can further enhance your grasp of tail recursion.

Take, for example, the classic problem of calculating the factorial of a number. Consider a standard recursive approach:

```
FUNCTION factorial(n):
    IF n == 1:
        RETURN 1
    ELSE:
        RETURN n * factorial(n-1)
```

This function will compute $n!$ correctly, but it isn't tail-recursive because the last action multiplies n with the factorial of n-1.

Let's convert this into a tail-recursive function:

```
FUNCTION tailRecursiveFactorial(n, a=1):
    IF n == 0:
```

```
      RETURN a
   ELSE:
      RETURN tailRecursiveFactorial(n-1, n*a)
```

In this function, we introduced an accumulator argument `a` that accumulates the product of all numbers from `n` down to 1. So, instead of waiting for the result of `factorial(n-1)`, we calculate the product `n*a` first and pass it to the next recursive call.

What we achieved is a function capable of handling larger factorial calculations more effectively compared to the standard recursive function. This leads us directly into discussing a key aspect of tail recursion: optimization.

6.3. Optimization and Tail Call Optimization (TCO)

This unique habit of tail recursion—reusing the same stack frame for recursive function calls—has spurred a compiler optimization technique, fittingly dubbed Tail Call Optimization (TCO).

The logic is simple and compelling. If a function call is the last operation within a function, why not reuse the stack frame instead of creating a new one? The compiler can replace the current activation record (the informatic structure supporting local variables, return values, and such) with the new one, essentially transforming the recursion into an iteration.

However, not all languages support TCO. Particularly, it's mostly supported in functional programming languages due to their heavy reliance on recursive operations. Languages like JavaScript have had a tumultuous history with TCO, currently not supporting it as of ES2020. Meanwhile, Python also lacks support for TCO, and Java only partially supports it—accredited to the risk of potential StackOverflowErrors.

Here's how a Tail Call Optimized version of our factorial function will
look:

```
FUNCTION tco_factorial(n, a=1):
    IF n == 0:
        RETURN a
    ELSE:
        REPLACETOPSTACKFRAMEWITH tco_factorial(n-1, n*a)
```

In this case, REPLACETOPSTACKFRAMEWITH isn't a real command, but it's a
theoretical construct replacing the current stack frame with the new
recursive call instead of adding a new one.

6.4. Conclusion

By now, you should possess an intact understanding of tail recursion
and its potential for optimization. The ability to convert regular
recursion into tail recursion certainly broadens the optimization
prospects for any programmer. The more you practice recursion and
understand the beauty of TCO, the better you can write efficient,
cleaner, and faster programs.

Remember, understanding tail recursion isn't just an exercise in
academic fulfillment. It's an essential tool in your programming
arsenal that, once mastered, can yield efficient solutions operating
within optimum space and time complexities.

Stay tuned to the next chapter where we will unbox 'Recursion in
Data Structures' to explore how recursion finds practical application,
demonstrating the formidable prowess of recursive algorithms.

Happy Recursing!

Chapter 7. Divide & Conquer: Recursion in Algorithmic Problem Solving

In the riveting journey of recursion, an essential stop is the strategy of Divide and Conquer. This, in essence, is the act of breaking a larger problem into smaller, easily solvable parts, hence standing true to its name. The simplicity of solving these parts, when in isolation, amplifies the appeal of this technique significantly.

7.1. Unveiling the Strategy of Divide and Conquer

The strategy of Divide and Conquer consists of three distinct steps:

1. Divide: The first step requires you to fragment the problem into smaller subproblems. The nature of these subproblems is such that they mirror the original problem structure but are of a reduced size.

2. Conquer: Then, we proceed to solve these subproblems individually. A crucial aspect here is that these subproblems are usually solved independently.

3. Merge: Eventually, we bring together the solutions of the subproblems to construct a solution for the overall problem.

More often than not, a recursive approach is embraced to solve these sub-problems, pointing towards the intertwining relationship between recursion and Divide and Conquer. We recognize the recursive nature in the divide step when the original problem is continuously divided until a base case is reached. The problem is then solved in the conquer step, and solutions are recursively put together in the merge step.

However, as with any technique, the implementation is often less straightforward than the theory, a statement true for Divide and Conquer as well. Let's understand it in more detail with an example.

7.2. The Epitome of Divide and Conquer: The Merge Sort Algorithm

One of the most iconic examples of the application of the Divide and Conquer in Recursive programming is the Merge Sort Algorithm. The pseudocode below demonstrates how this strategy can be applied effectively:

```
MERGE_SORT(A)
1. If the length(A) <= 1, return A
2. Midpoint = length(A) / 2
3. Left = MERGE_SORT(A[0 ... Midpoint - 1])
4. Right = MERGE_SORT(A[Midpoint ... length(A) - 1])
5. Return MERGE(Left, Right)
```

The Merge Sort Algorithm applies the Divide and Conquer strategy as follows:

1. Divide: The array is divided into two halves.

2. Conquer: The merge sort is applied recursively on both halves of the array.

3. Merge: The two sorted halves are merged to form a sorted array.

This example underlines why Divide and Conquer is hailed as a powerful method in Recursive Programming. The fact that the original problem (sorting the entire array) has been distilled into smaller, identical problems (sorting the halves) means that a recursive approach was naturally followed.

7.3. Setting the Stage: Base Cases and Recursive Cases

Working in consonance with the Divide and Conquer technique is the concept of base cases and recursive cases.

1. Base Case: This refers to the most fundamental form of the problem, where no further division can occur. In the above Merge Sort example, an array of length $\Leftarrow 1$ is the base case since no more division is possible. Identifying a base case is critical, as this prevents infinite recursion.

2. Recursive Case: This is a version of the problem that contains within itself smaller instances of the same problem. The recursive case propels us towards the base case.

Understanding how your algorithm handles base and recursive cases requires a deep comprehension of problem structure. Cracking the Recursive Cases and Base Cases is often synonymous with having cracked the problem.

Our journey around recursion would be incomplete without exploring its costs and benefits relative to other programming techniques. So, let's dig in.

7.4. Recursion and Memory: A Trade-Off to Consider

Recursion, although incredibly powerful, is not always the go-to programming strategy. One key factor is that recursions store state information. With each recursion, the method's context (including local variables and parameters) is saved onto the system stack to be restored upon returning.

If an algorithm involves deep recursion (i.e., a high number of recursive calls), the system stack can fill up quickly, leading to a potential stack overflow. Therefore, understanding your system's stack limit and the recursive depth your algorithm may reach is crucial.

7.5. Unraveling Tail Recursion

For many programmers, a strategy to combat the relative memory inefficiency of recursive calls is Tail Recursion. Here, any computation is performed at the start, before the recursive call is made. The result of each recursive call and the associated state information is immediately returned, reducing the need to push and pop off the system call stack.

This contrasts with non-tail recursive calls, where calculations occur after the recursive call, meaning more information is stored and released from the stack, consuming more memory.

While tail recursion does improve upon the memory usage of recursion, it may not always be applicable and depends strongly on problem structure.

7.6. Wrapping It Up

In a nutshell, the Divide and Conquer strategy using recursion is a formidable tool in a programmer's arsenal. The tangible advantage of breaking complex problems into manageable chunks is immeasurable. While it does come with memory concerns, with a good understanding of your problem's structure and your system's limitations, you can optimize and balance it effectively.

In the world of recursion, the seeming simplicity masks the

simmering power beneath. The beauty of this fascinating trait is revealed only when one delves deep into it, unafraid to navigate its labyrinthine nuances. Patience and practice remain the key, as with any new skill; however, rest assured that the power unleashed by mastering recursion will make the investment worthwhile. Indeed, the world of advanced coding becomes infinitely more exhilarating with recursion at your fingertips.

Chapter 8. Advanced Recursive Patterns

Before we plunge into the depths of advanced recursive patterns, it's best we revisit the foundational concept of recursion. By definition, recursion is a coding methodology where a function calls itself to solve a smaller part of the overall problem. This fundamental idea powers many algorithms integral to higher coding techniques.

8.1. Understanding the Base Case

In recursion, a critical concept is the base case. It is so named because it forms the base, or the stopping point, of any recursion. The absence of a base case can lead to infinite recursion, which can crash your program. Understanding your base case is an absolute requirement before you set out any recursion adventure.

Here's a representation of a simple recursion where the function `factorial(n)` calculates the factorial of a number:

```
function factorial(n) {
    if (n === 0) {
      return 1;
    } else {
      return n * factorial(n-1);
    }
}
```

The base case in this simple function is `n === 0`, at which point it stops calling itself recursively. This understanding will form the bedrock as more complex examples come later on.

8.2. Recursive Tree

To develop the knack for solving complicated recursion problems, visualizing recursion in the form of a recursive tree is a helpful practice. Nodes of this tree represent the recursive calls, and its structure manifests the execution of these calls. Observing this tree, we notice a pattern known as the "recursive leap of faith"—we assume that recursion correctly solves the smaller subproblem. So, we break down the problem into smaller chunks until we reach a point where no further breakdown is needed (i.e., the base case).

8.3. The Two Forms of Recursion

Recursion typically operates in two ways:

1. **Head recursion**: The recursive call is executed before other operations in the function.

```
function headRecursion(n) {
    if (n > 0) {
        headRecursion(n-1);
        console.log(n);
    }
}
```

1. **Tail recursion**: The recursive call is executed after all other operations in the function.

```
function tailRecursion(n) {
    if (n > 0) {
        console.log(n);
        tailRecursion(n-1);
    }
```

```
    }
```

Mastering the difference between the two opens the door to understanding more advanced recursion patterns.

8.4. Multiple Recursive Calls

Not all recursive functions are as straightforward as the `factorial(n)` example. Some algorithms require making more than one recursive call in the function. An excellent example is the Fibonacci sequence generator.

```
function fibonacci(n) {
    if (n <= 1)
        return n;
    else
        return fibonacci(n-1) + fibonacci(n-2);
}
```

In this example, the function calls itself twice, each time with a different parameter. This allows the calculation of the Fibonacci sequence, a classic example of multiple recursive calls. It demands a more in-depth understanding of recursive function flow, and a higher degree of visualization.

8.5. Space and Time Complexity in Recursive Algorithms

Just as with iterative algorithms, computing the space and time complexity of recursive algorithms is critical. The time complexity is often directly proportional to the number of recursive calls, while the space complexity is related to the maximum depth of the recursion tree.

However, not every recursive algorithm is efficient. For instance, the Fibonacci sequence generator is highly inefficient due to its excessive duplicate computations. To enhance it, we can introduce the technique of dynamic programming.

8.6. Dynamic Programming and Memoization

We can optimize recursive algorithms by implementing dynamic programming. It employs a technique called memoization, where we store the results of expensive function calls and reuse them when necessary, avoiding the need for redundant operations.

Here's our Fibonacci sequence generator with memoization:

```
function fib(n, memo = {}) {
    if (n <= 1) return n;
    if (!memo[n]) {
        memo[n] = fib(n - 1, memo) + fib(n - 2, memo);
    }
    return memo[n];
}
```

This optimized version vastly reduces both space and time complexity by eliminating redundant computations.

8.7. Backtracking

Backtracking is an algorithmic technique that solves problems recursively by trying to build a solution incrementally. It removes solutions that fail to satisfy the constraints of the problem at any point of time (by time, here, is referred to the time elapsed till that point).

A classic example of backtracking is the eight queens puzzle, where eight queens should be placed on an 8x8 chess board such that no two queens threaten each other.

8.8. Understanding Recursive Paradigms

Mastering recursion requires understanding the common paradigms. Whether it's the concept of "Divide and Conquer", where a problem is divided into subproblems, solved independently, and combined to form the final solution, or "Decrease and Conquer", where we decrease the problem size at each step and solve the smaller problem directly. Understanding these paradigms can be a competitive edge in manipulating recursion.

8.9. Exploring Recursive Traversals and Searches

Recursive traversals are commonly used for data structures like trees and graphs. Tree traversal techniques such as Pre-Order, In-Order, Post-Order, and Level-Order Traversals are some examples. Additionally, graph traversal or searching techniques like Depth-First Search (DFS) and Breadth-First Search (BFS) use recursion.

With this understanding of recursive patterns explored above, you're now on the path of mastering recursion. Remember, like all things in programming, practice is key. It's time to put hands to keyboard and weave the elegance of recursion into your code, making it more efficient, more brilliant.

Chapter 9. Real-world Applications of Recursion

While recursion is a concept shrouded in an aura of complexity, it lends itself to a multitude of real-world applications. These applications span an array of diverse fields and disciplines, showcasing the versatility of this advanced coding paradigm. In this chapter, we will dive deep into some of its noteworthy applications and explore how to implement them in code.

9.1. Mathematical Problems

One of the most common applications of recursion is in solving mathematical problems. Recursive algorithms provide a straightforward way of implementing complex mathematical operations by breaking them down into simpler, solvable components.

9.1.1. Factorial

A factorial, represented as n!, is the product of all positive integers up to n. The recursive function to find the factorial of a number n can be written as follows:

```python
def factorial(n):
    if n == 1:
        return 1
    else:
        return n * factorial(n-1)
```

Note how the function calls itself (hence, recursion) to calculate the factorials of all preceding numbers until it reaches 1, at which point it begins to unravel and multiply these values together.

9.1.2. Fibonacci Series

The Fibonacci series is a sequence of numbers such that each number is the sum of the two preceding ones, usually starting with 0 and 1. This problem is also efficiently solved using recursion.

```
def fibonacci(n):
    if n <= 1:
        return n
    else:
        return (fibonacci(n-1) + fibonacci(n-2))
```

9.2. Search Algorithms

Recursion is an integral part of several search algorithms, particularly Depth-First Search (DFS) and Binary Search.

9.2.1. Depth-First Search

DFS is an algorithm for traversing or searching tree or graph data structures. It works by diving deep into a graph, following a single path until it reaches the end before retracing its steps and exploring other paths.

```
def DFS(graph, start, visited = None):
    if visited is None:
        visited = set()
    visited.add(start)
    for next in graph[start] - visited:
        DFS(graph, next, visited)
    return visited
```

9.2.2. Binary Search

Binary Search is an efficient algorithm for finding an item from a sorted list of items. It works by repeatedly dividing the search interval by half. If the sought value is less than the item in the middle of the interval, narrow the interval to the first half. Otherwise, narrow it to the second half.

```python
def binary_search(arr, low, high, x):
    if high >= low:
        mid = (high + low) // 2
        if arr[mid] == x:
            return mid
        elif arr[mid] > x:
            return binary_search(arr, low, mid - 1, x)
        else:
            return binary_search(arr, mid + 1, high, x)
    else:
        return -1
```

9.3. Fractals

Fractals are intricate geometric shapes that are self-similar, meaning they can be divided into parts, each of which is a reduced-scale copy of the whole. Fractals are naturally recursive, making them an ideal illustration of recursion's power.

9.3.1. Koch Snowflake

The Koch Snowflake, a classic example of a fractal, can be generated using recursion. Each iteration of the recursion refines the edges of the shape, adding more detail.

```python
def koch_snowflake(order, size):
```

```
    if order == 0:
        forward(size)
    else:
        for angle in [60, -120, 60, 0]:
            koch_snowflake(order-1, size/3)
            left(angle)
```

9.4. Data Structures

Recursion also plays a significant role in manipulating and managing
certain data structures, notably in trees and linked lists.

9.4.1. Binary Trees

In a binary tree data structure, each node has at most two children,
referred to as the left child and the right child. One can traverse these
trees using recurison.

```
def preorder_traversal(root):
    if root:
        print(root)
        preorder_traversal(root.left)
        preorder_traversal(root.right)
```

9.4.2. Linked Lists

A linked list is a linear data structure where each element points to
the next. Recursion can be used to traverse, search, and even reverse
a linked list.

```
def recursive_search(node, data):
    if node is None:
        return False
```

```python
    if node.data == data:
        return True
    return recursive_search(node.next, data)
```

These are just a few of the myriad ways recursion can be used to
solve both intricate and day-to-day problems, serving as a critical tool
in any programmer's toolkit. As you unravel the intricacies of
recursion, you'll find yourself harnessing its power to render
complex problems solvable, and in doing so, reinventing the very
way you approach programming.

Chapter 10. Infinite Recursion: Risks, Issues and Solutions

As you delve deeper into the world of recursion, you may come across an exotic yet intimidating concept—Infinite Recursion. Like a loop that reverberates endlessly, this scenario can send chills down the spine of any developer. But fear not, for in this segment, we dissect infinite recursion, pore over its risks and issues, and indicate practical steps to address and evade this potential coding trap.

10.1. Understanding Infinite Recursion

Before we discuss solutions, it is crucial to first recognize and understand infinite recursion. In essence, it's a scenario where a recursive function calls itself indefinitely without a terminating condition. This is similar to an infinite loop in iterative programming.

Imagine being in front of two mirrors, one behind you and one in front. As the mirrors reflect each other, an infinite corridor of reflections is created. This can serve as a metaphor for infinite recursion where a function, instead of terminating, continues calling itself creating an endless chain of function calls.

```
function infiniteRecursion() {
    infiniteRecursion(); // infinite recursion here
}
infiniteRecursion();
```

The problem lies not only in the infinite execution but also in the ever-growing consumption of stack memory, as each function call is added to the call stack. This can lead to a stack overflow error, causing the program to crash.

10.2. The Perils of Infinite Recursion

The pitfalls of infinite recursion stretch further than first may appear. Here are the primary risks evolved around this issue:

- **System Resource Consumption:** Each recursive call consumes stack space. When the function calls itself infinitely, the stack grows until it eventually overflows, causing the program to crash. This overconsumption of resources can paralyze other concurrent processes, potentially compromising the system's performance.

- **Immeasurable Execution Time:** Infinite recursion can lead to unresponsive programs due to the indefinite function calls, which can be especially problematic in real-time systems where response time is critical.

- **Debugging Difficulty:** Infinite recursion can make code debugging more complex. Identifying the root cause or the iteration causing the problem characteristically challenges even seasoned developers.

10.3. Spotting Infinite Recursion

Key signs can indicate potential infinite recursion. Primarily, if a recursive function does not have a well-defined base case or the base case is improperly used, infinite recursion is often the result. Monitoring system resources and identifying sudden unnecessary upticks in usage—especially RAM consumption—can guide you towards stemming the tide of infinite recursion. Profiling tools can help spot unusual spikes in resource consumption, hinting towards problematic areas in code.

10.4. Mitigating the Risks

Now let's focus on techniques and best practices to prevent and handle infinite recursive cases:

- **Establish a Robust Base Case:** Start by defining a robust base case that effectively terminates recursion. Ensure that for every recursive function, it reaches this base case in all possible scenarios.

```python
def factorial(n):
    if n == 1:      # base case
        return 1
    else:
        return n * factorial(n - 1)
```

This factorial function is a good example, where `n == 1` is a robust base case, ensuring termination.

- **Limit Recursion Depth:** In certain programming languages like Python, you can set a limit to the recursion depth. Although not a solution in itself, it helps prevent crashing the code through a stack overflow error.

```python
import sys
sys.setrecursionlimit(1000)
```

- **Iterative Backups:** In certain scenarios, it's viable to rewrite recursive functions as iterative functions using popular loop constructs. It will eliminate the risk of stack overflow and make the function's space complexity O(1) instead of O(n).

```python
def factorial_iterative(n):
```

```
    result = 1
    for i in range(1, n + 1):
        result *= i
    return result
```

Here the factorial function has been rewritten iteratively, completely discarding the risk of infinite recursion.

- **Use Tail Recursion (Where Supported):** Some languages, like Scheme or Haskell, support tail recursion, which significantly minimizes the risk of stack overflow and infinite recursion.

Remember, although powerful and magical recursion may seem, it's critical to keep its beastly counterpart, infinite recursion, in check. As we grapple these concepts with careful regard, we begin to unlock the full potential of this advanced programming technique, casting away the shrouds of fear and uncertainty. And by understanding the risks, issues, and solutions related to infinite recursion, you are another essential step closer to mastering recursion.

Chapter 11. Looking Ahead: Recursion in Contemporary Programming Languages

Recursion, as a concept, is a prevalent characteristic across virtually all programming languages, albeit with variant implementations. Its ability to simplify complex problems and create efficient solutions makes recursion a must-have tool in the arsenal of any programmer. To truly appreciate its ubiquity, we turn our gaze towards how recursion is implemented in contemporary programming languages—Java, C++, JavaScript, Python, and Haskell.

11.1. Java and Recursion

Let's explore the relationship between Java and Recursion. A statically typed, object-oriented language, Java provides robust support for recursion. Here's an example of a recursive factorial function:

```
public static int factorial(int n) {
    if (n <= 1) {
        return 1;
    } else {
        return n * factorial(n - 1);
    }
}
```

In the above code, we can observe that Java recursion works in a top-down manner. It starts by solving the bigger problem and then carries out the smaller sub-problems.

Moreover, Java also supports Tail Recursion, but it lacks significant optimization. Due to the lack of Tail Call Optimization (TCO), using recursion for large inputs can lead to a stack overflow error. Ideal use cases include traversing tree or graph structures and solving smaller-scope problems.

11.2. C++ and Recursion

C implements recursion in a manner similar to Java. It's a statically typed, multi-paradigm language that readily supports recursion. Here's an example of a recursive Fibonacci function in C.

```c
int fibonacci(int n) {
    if(n == 0) {
        return 0;
    } else if(n == 1) {
        return 1;
    } else {
        return fibonacci(n-1) + fibonacci(n-2);
    }
}
```

C recursion follows a top-down execution. It also supports Tail Recursion and contains compiler optimizations for it. You can force Tail Call Optimization (TCO) in C using the GNU Compiler Collection (GCC), albeit with substantial complexities involved. Similar to Java, ideal use cases involve computational operations and traversal of hierarchically structured data.

11.3. JavaScript and Recursion

Moving away from statically typed languages, we enter the realm of dynamically typed languages starting with JavaScript. JavaScript's relationship with recursion is intricate. JavaScript handles recursion in a similar vein to other languages. Here's the same factorial function implemented in JavaScript:

```javascript
function factorial(n) {
    if(n <= 1) {
        return 1;
    } else {
        return n * factorial(n - 1);
    }
}
```

Unfortunately, earlier versions of ECMAScript envisioned JavaScript as a light scripting language. As a result, it lacks native support for Tail Call Optimization (TCO), which can make recursive solutions inefficient for significant input sizes. However, subsequent updates (ES6) planned to address this issue, but practical compatibility across environments is still hit-or-miss.

11.4. Python and Recursion

Let's move over to Python, a high-level, dynamically typed language known for its simplicity and elegance. Yes, you guessed it right, Python supports recursion too. To illustrate, let's write a recursive function to compute the nth number in a Fibonacci sequence.

```python
def fibonacci(n):
    if n <= 0:
        return 0
    elif n == 1:
        return 1
    else:
        return fibonacci(n-1) + fibonacci(n-2)
```

Python handles recursion in a non-optimized manner. It has a low recursion depth limit (set at 1000 by default), impacting efficient use of recursion for larger input sizes. This limitation is a preventative measure against Python's lack of Tail Call Optimization—which should be mitigated by using iterative solutions or other non-recursive approaches in Python for larger problems.

11.5. Haskell and Recursion

Last but not least, we examine Haskell, a statically typed, purely functional language, and its handling of recursion. In Haskell, recursion is not merely an added tool. Instead, it's often the first and most natural solution to most problems in functional programming. Here's how a factorial function looks in Haskell:

```
factorial :: Integer -> Integer
factorial 0 = 1
factorial n = n * factorial (n - 1)
```

Haskell supports recursion intrinsically, and its performance gets further boosted by powerful features like lazy evaluation and Tail Call Optimization. These features make recursion a primary and efficient construct for problem-solving in Haskell.

In summary, recursion is a powerful technique universally applicable across different programming languages, each with its nuances and considerations. Mastering recursion involves gaining insight into not only its theoretical background but also its practical implementation in various languages. It's crucial to be aware of its limitations too, like maximum depth and efficiency with large inputs, to utilize recursion optimally. Remember—the more adept you become at using recursion, the more complex problems you'll be able to decompose and resolve effectively. Happy coding!